Support Staff in Schools
Promoting the emotional and
social development of children
and young people

Vanessa Cooper

national
children's
bureau

NCB promotes the voices, interests and well-being of all children and young people across every aspect of their lives.

As an umbrella body for the children's sector in England and Northern Ireland, NCB provides essential information on policy, research and best practice for our members and other partners.

NCB aims to:

- challenge disadvantage in childhood
- work with children and young people to ensure they are involved in all matters that affect their lives
- promote multidisciplinary cross-agency partnerships and good practice
- influence government policy through policy development and advocacy
- undertake high quality research and work from an evidence-based perspective
- disseminate information to all those working with children and young people, and to children and young people themselves.

NCB has adopted and works within the UN Convention on the Rights of the Child.

Published by the National Children's Bureau

National Children's Bureau, 8 Wakley Street, London EC1V 7QE
Tel: 020 7843 6000
Website: www.ncb.org.uk
Registered charity number: 258825

© National Children's Bureau 2005

ISBN 1 904787 52 5

British Library Cataloguing in Publication Data
A catalogue record for this book is available from the British Library

The views expressed in this book are those of the authors and not necessarily those of the National Children's Bureau

Contents

Acknowledgements

Thanks to all those involved in the development work for this project including:

Jane Ayshford
Lesley Bolle
Paula Cain
Shazia Chaudry
Anthony Cox
Linda Disney
Julie Flett
Alison Gauld
Della Gawthorne
Veronica Harnett
Avril Haworth
Carol James
Cheryl Ladeatte
Julia Neal
Margaret Stockton
Teus Young

A special thank you to all the young people whose views and ideas have helped to shape this book. Finally, thanks to Tracey Anderson and Lana Hashem for administrative support.

Introduction

Why extra support is needed

Without the learning mentor and the Connexions worker, I would have got in a lot of trouble. I'd probably have been thrown out by now.
Girl, Year 9

For many children and young people, there are significant barriers to learning at school. They need extra help to be able to make the most of what education has to offer. Their difficulties may arise for many different reasons: problems at home, emotional trauma, abuse, low self-esteem, bereavement, bullying, learning difficulties, speaking English as an additional language or poverty. A well-planned programme of Personal Social and Health Education (PSHE) and Citizenship alongside pastoral care, taking place within a supportive ethos, will help most children and young people. However, for some the help needed is not simply more or better teaching, but the kind of one-to-one support for their social and emotional development which is beyond the curriculum focus, role, skills and capacity of some teachers.

In recognition of this, and as part of the move towards inclusive education, many schools have employed learning mentors, Connexions personal advisors (PAs) and a range of other support staff. These roles were established to raise the achievement of vulnerable children and young people by addressing personal, social and emotional issues which may act as barriers to learning.

More recently, the Green Paper *Every Child Matters* (DfES 2003a) and the subsequent Children Act have set out proposals for extending the workforce in schools to meet the needs of these children and young people. By bringing in relevant professionals to provide support for vulnerable children and young people, teachers will be freed up to concentrate on what they have been trained to do – teach. It is envisaged that these extended schools, with multidisciplinary teams of workers supporting children, young people and families, will be at the heart of many communities.

However, these ideas challenge some of the established roles of teaching staff and have prompted the need to consider how support staff and teaching staff can best work together to promote the personal, social and emotional development of children and young people.

The Children Act (2004) sets out five outcomes for children and young people that all who work with them should be working towards:

- **being healthy:** enjoying good physical and mental health and living a healthy lifestyle
- **staying safe:** being protected from harm and neglect
- **enjoying and achieving:** getting the most out of life and developing the skills for adulthood
- **making a positive contribution:** being involved with the community and society and not engaging in anti-social or offending behaviour
- **economic well-being:** not being prevented by economic disadvantage from achieving their full potential in life.

Aims of this book

This book shows how the work of support staff such as Connexions PAs and learning mentors can help schools to support children's emotional and social development. It looks at what schools need to do to make the most effective use of support staff and provides practical examples where this is already happening.

The principles contained in this book, and the examples of good practice, apply to the work of any professional involved in PSHE, Citizenship and pastoral care.

How the book is laid out

Section 1 defines what we mean by emotional and social development and why it is important.

Section 2 focuses on the roles of learning mentors and Connexions PAs. It explores the potential gains, to schools and to children and young people, of having access to specialist support workers in addition to the pastoral care provided by teaching staff.

Section 3 examines some of the issues that arise with these new roles in schools, setting out what makes support services successful and looking at potential barriers and how to deal with them.

Section 4 gives examples of good practice from around England.

Section 5 sets out a checklist for effective practice in the provision of support services in schools for children and young people.

What did the project involve?

The project which informed this book involved meetings with:

- service managers
- teachers
- learning mentors
- Connexions PAs
- children and young people in primary and secondary schools across England.

A request for information was issued and examples of good practice were collected through the National Children's Bureau's PSHE and Citizenship email network.

A national consultation seminar also took place, which was attended by PSHE and Citizenship advisors, Healthy Schools coordinators, primary care team staff, Connexions staff, learning mentors and young people.

Who is this book for?

This book is for policy-makers at local, regional and national levels, enabling them to take stock of what has been achieved by introducing Connexions PAs and learning mentors in schools, and what this means for the provision of support services in schools.

It will also be a useful tool for inclusion teams and Healthy Schools Partnerships, helping to raise awareness of the support worker's role as part of a whole-school approach to personal, social, emotional and behavioural issues.

Senior management teams in schools will find Sections 2, 3 and 4 helpful in providing guidance on how the role of support staff might be developed most effectively in their school.

Learning mentors, Connexions PAs and other support workers will find Section 4 a useful source of ideas.

1 Why promote emotional and social development?

There is growing recognition that children and young people's emotional and social development affects their ability to learn. Research into the way that the brain works suggests that effective learning can only take place when people experience emotional well-being (NHSS 2004b). It is no surprise to most people that, as Daniel Goleman (1995) says, 'Students who are anxious, angry or depressed don't learn.' Relationships with others will, of course, affect an individual's emotional state, and children and young people who are having problems with relationships at home or at school are likely to be in a highly charged emotional state.

Schools, therefore, need to pay attention to their pupils' emotional and social development in order to help them learn and achieve. In recognition of this, the National Healthy Schools Programme has produced guidance on promoting emotional health and well-being (NHSS 2004b); and the Department for Education and Skills (DfES) has produced materials for supporting children in the emotional and social aspects of learning in primary and secondary school. The DfES has also published a research report on personal and social development on behalf of the Connexions Service National Unit (2003). The report considers theories of personal development and sets out the characteristics of effective provision in youth and support services.

There is a range of core emotional and social skills necessary for healthy emotional and social development and for the capacity to engage effectively with education. These include:

- empathy with others
- a positive sense of self
- an understanding of how emotions impact on behaviour and beliefs
- an understanding of rights and responsibilities
- acceptance of diversity and difference
- a willingness to participate in society.

PSHE and Citizenship play a major role in the school's capacity to help children and young people develop these qualities. They are also a key strategy for creating an inclusive school which supports and values all children, including those with emotional and social difficulties. Effective PSHE and Citizenship includes three essential elements:

- the acquisition of accessible, relevant and age-appropriate information
- the clarification and development of attitudes and values that support self-esteem and are positive to health and well-being
- the development of personal and social skills to enable emotional development and interaction with others, the making of positive health choices and active participation in society, as well as the ability to access help and support services (NCB 2003).

The early development and experiences of some children and young people are influenced by a range of negative factors which can inhibit their emotional well-being and resilience as they grow up. These include the lack of a positive, consistent relationship with a caring adult; family breakdown; parents with an alcohol or drug problem or a mental illness (or both); violence in the home; poverty; lack of firm, consistent discipline; and lack of home support for education. For other children, a range of experiences may impact on their emotional state and ability to make effective relationships. These include loss through separation, divorce or bereavement; being fostered, adopted or transferred to public care; being bullied; arriving in the United Kingdom as an asylum seeker or refugee; and being excluded from school.

Effective schools find ways of providing extra support for those who need it, through one-to-one and small group support, within the context of an overall commitment to promoting emotional and social development. To do this effectively over the long term they will need to develop effective ways of establishing and managing the role of support staff.

2 Support staff – who they are and how they can help

Support staff include all those professionals working in schools to support pastoral care and promote children and young people's personal, social and emotional development. They include learning mentors, Connexions PAs, youth workers, educational welfare officers, drugs and sexual health workers, counsellors, educational psychologists, child and adolescent mental health services (CAMHS) staff, business and other mentors and staff from voluntary organisations. They may be part of the school staff team or they may come into the school from outside agencies.

Some background information about the newer roles of learning mentors and Connexions PAs is given below.

Learning mentors are one of the strands of the Excellence in Cities (EiC) programme, a package of measures designed to improve inner-city education. Introduced in 1999, it has been extended to 57 local education authorities (LEAs) and 44 smaller excellence clusters. Learning mentors are employed directly by primary and secondary schools and work with children and young people who are at risk of underachieving or disengaging with education. They work on a one-to-one or group basis. A key role is to 'signpost' specialist support agencies in the community. They have been recruited from a wide range of backgrounds including social workers, youth workers, police officers, educational welfare officers and existing school support and administrative staff. They undergo a basic five-day induction programme organised nationally and complete a portfolio of evidence to be accredited.

The Connexions Service was established in 2000 to provide integrated advice, guidance and access to personal development opportunities for 14- to 19-year-olds. Connexions offers a universal service of personal advisors (PAs) based in schools who can assist with choosing courses and careers, including access to broader personal development through sporting, creative and volunteering activities. Other PAs are based in other youth settings and target young people who are not in education, employment or training. They can also provide help and advice on issues such as drugs, sexual health and homelessness. PAs are employed by the local Connexions Partnership and are likely to work in several schools in an area. Many were transferred from former roles as careers advisors but some have been recruited from the youth service or other backgrounds. PAs must have an appropriate professional qualification to at least NVQ level 4 or equivalent in a relevant professional discipline, and have studied for the new Diploma for Personal Advisors or the Understanding Connexions course.

The newly developed Occupational Standards for Learning, Development and Support Services integrate qualifications for educational welfare officers, Connexions PAs and learning mentors, and will lead to NVQ qualifications at NVQ levels 3 and 4.

For the purposes of this book, and for the sake of brevity, all these roles will be referred to as support staff or support workers.

Why have support staff in schools?

In the past, some schools have found funding for and appointed their own counsellors or other support staff. In the USA, Scotland and other countries it is common for schools to have guidance counsellors on-site. The introduction of Connexions PAs and learning mentors into schools is the first significant opportunity that schools in England have had for planned, centrally funded staff who do not have teaching commitments and who have a remit for inclusion and removing barriers to learning.

Headteachers and other teachers have responded very positively to these new additions to their workforce:

They [learning mentors] are not tied to a timetable, so if there's a crisis there's always someone available. We would have lost some children if it hadn't been for the learning mentors, we would never have kept them on board.
Deputy head, secondary school

For some pupils, it makes a huge difference if someone like a learning mentor is there just to say hello in the mornings.
Deputy head, secondary school

Children and young people, too, clearly appreciate the distinct role of learning mentors and Connexions PAs and the kind of support that they can give.

Learning mentors are there to help when someone has a problem like with bullying.
Girl, Year 10

Without the learning mentor and PA I would have been kicked out for fighting and anger problems. I've got a short fuse.
Boy, Year 9

Their benefits have also been recognised by the Office for Standards in Education (Ofsted):

Learning mentors are making a significant effect on the attendance, behaviour, self-esteem and progress of the pupils they support ... the most successful and highly valued strand of the EiC programme ... In 95 per cent of the survey schools, inspectors judged that the mentoring programme made a positive contribution to the mainstream provision of the school as a whole, and had a beneficial effect on the behaviour of individual pupils and on their ability to learn and make progress (Ofsted 2003a).
Ofsted

[Connexions] Partnerships focus their intervention very effectively on disaffected pupils and are overcoming the complex needs of some young people so that they can re-engage with education (Ofsted 2004).
Ofsted

The National Foundation for Educational Research (NFER) interim evaluation reports on Excellence in Cities (NFER 2003) also underline the continuing success of learning mentors and have identified positive outcomes for students as well as for the school as a whole. They report that outcomes for children and young people include improvements in:

- behaviour
- attitudes
- self-confidence
- self-esteem
- attendance
- exclusion rates.

They report that outcomes for the school include:

- reducing the workload of senior staff
- developing relationships with parents
- providing for all pupils
- providing an alternative viewpoint on pupils' behaviour.

Key benefits

As a result of the meetings, the interviews with staff, children and young people and the visits to schools carried out for this project, the following features emerged as the key benefits of having support workers such as Connexions PAs and learning mentors in schools.

Time and expertise for pastoral care

Support workers such as Connexions PAs and learning mentors take work off the hands of teachers whose non-teaching time is limited, and they also bring a range of skills and expertise to deal with the various problems that they encounter. Support workers are trained to identify individuals and groups of children and young people who are vulnerable and require support and guidance, to assess their needs and 'to signpost' them to sources of further help if necessary. In one school, learning mentors are taking on the role of heads of year.

They have time to listen – teachers don't have the time.
Pupil, Battersea Park Technology College

The capacity to offer children one-to-one or very small group sessions means that support workers can focus on individual needs and plan support programmes that target those needs. Both learning mentors and Connexions PAs work with children and young people to set their own targets and reflect on how well they are doing.

What learning mentors do is tailored to suit you as an individual not as a group.
Girl, Year 10

They can give some very individual advice and support.
Girl, Year 10

Contacts with local agencies

A key role of both Connexions PAs and learning mentors is to establish links with a range of organisations in the local community and to work in partnership with them. They have time during the working day to contact people from other agencies and to attend partnership groups, such as teenage pregnancy advisory groups or drug reference groups, and so are able to keep schools in touch with developments. Schools have benefited from multi-agency curriculum enrichment days, and outside visitors who help with PSHE and Citizenship, as well as the increased range of support services available to pupils – all organised by support workers.

Because they come from outside the school they have links in the community.
Girl, Year 10

The positive thing about Connexions is that they can look outside the school; they bring an awareness of the local community; they can be impartial; they can liaise with a huge number of different agencies.
Connexions manager

A different relationship with pupils

Without the necessity of having to work to a fixed curriculum and daily timetable, support workers can focus on the needs of individuals in a more relaxed and informal setting than the classroom. The focus of their work is on how individual pupils are progressing. As one Connexions PA put it, 'I can see things from the pupils' point of view'. A teacher added:

Sometimes it seems like the support staff have got all the best bits of working with our students.

The children and young people interviewed were clearly aware of the difference.

They're not like teachers. You can talk to them like friends. They're more open, more confidential, relaxed, have jokes with them.
Boy, Year 9

He's really friendly – not like a strict teacher. You can get more personal.
Girl, Year 9

If you tell a teacher that you haven't understood something, they say you weren't listening, [but] you **were** listening, and you just didn't get it. Mentors never say that, they just help you.
Boy, Year 10

Students agreed that they would prefer to talk to a PA or learning mentor about issues that they regarded as sensitive and personal.

The PA can give advice on sex and health better than a teacher.
Girl, Year 10

Trust and clarity about confidentiality

The young people we have worked with have more trust that the service provided by support workers, such as learning mentors and Connexions PAs, is confidential. Although teachers are in the position of being able to offer the same degree of confidentiality, it is clear that young people and teachers do not always understand this.

It's good because you can tell them [learning mentors] things and they won't tell anyone.
Boy, Year 9

Learning mentors keep confidentiality. They do not gossip.
Girl, Year 10

Scope to work outside the school

Support workers such as Connexions PAs and learning mentors have the capacity to go out of the school during the working day and in the evenings to meet parents, make home visits and to take groups of pupils on visits and school outings. These can include activities to extend their experience and build confidence, such as residential activities or visits to further education colleges, workplaces, clinics and other local services.

Seeing the child in the context of family and community

Support workers such as PAs and learning mentors, working with pupils on a one-to-one or small group basis, are able to find out what is happening in their lives in a way that teachers, working with whole classes at a time, find it hard to do. Family bereavements, divorce and parental illness are just a few of the events that can affect any child's ability to concentrate on school work. Support staff can be aware of these and act promptly, providing immediate support and referral to appropriate services if necessary.

We can take the time to find out about the pupil's background, their family etc. Without the learning mentors, the school might not know what's going on for young people.
Learning mentor, community college

Support staff can also provide an alternative perspective on a young person's behaviour and attitudes, and help other staff to see things from a young person's point of view.

I can take the young person's agenda to the school and advocate for them.
Connexions PA, community college

The NFER evaluations of Excellence in Cities (NFER 2003) point out that the presence of learning mentors in a school can also change the way teachers think about students with problems, saying that they have found that many teachers have learnt about the benefits of supporting students and have introduced a new way of working with them. They quote a teacher as saying, 'I've learned that you can get more out of pupils by not forcing them to work but by supporting them.' One PA who was previously a teacher said, 'As a teacher, I would just see pupils being difficult. Now I can help teachers see the bigger picture.'

Learning mentors can help teachers see pupils in a different light and then the pupils see themselves more positively.
Learning mentor, community college

Opportunities to reflect on teaching and learning

Many children and young people we talked to as part of this project commented on the way in which working with a Connexions PA or a learning mentor has helped them understand more about themselves as learners and how to cope in a busy classroom.

He [learning mentor] taught me if you show respect, you'll be respected back.
Pupil, high school

We did role plays to help me deal with situations with teachers and other pupils. Now I really know what to do and what not to do.
Pupil, high school

The NFER also confirms this:

Learning mentors had also helped students to improve the way they related to their teachers and peers through helping them to understand and communicate more effectively with others.

Young people also commented on the way they were helped to understand why education was important.

The PA helped me look into what I'm going to be doing in future. He gave me information about colleges, universities and courses and made me think about my future.
Boy, Year 9

Learning mentors can also help pupils to see their problems in a different light.

If they can have one or two good moments in the day with us, they can see themselves more positively.
Learning mentor, community college

Support tailored to the needs of children and communities

As can be seen from the examples of good practice in Section 4, support workers such as Connexions PAs and learning mentors can carry out their role in many different ways. Learning mentors, in particular, work with individuals, groups, families and even whole school communities, because their role is only loosely defined in terms of removing barriers to learning. Connexions PAs can also offer flexible provision: from universal careers education and guidance to intensive support for targeted pupils. In both cases, it seems that the universal provision informs and enhances targeted work. Children and young people get to know the worker in a general context and feel more comfortable accessing them for more personal support.

Connexions PAs and learning mentors sometimes have the opportunity to see their targeted pupils alongside other pupils. One learning mentor, who was involved in running a project with the whole of Year 8, said:

It's been brilliant to see **all** the kids and for them to see our room and our role.
Learning mentor, community college

Staff with a range of backgrounds and skills

The range of backgrounds from which support workers such as learning mentors and Connexions PAs are recruited means that they bring a wide range of skills and experience to bear on their current work. Their training means that they have knowledge of child and adolescent development, skills in providing a variety of support approaches as well as for organising out-of-school activities. These skills complement those of teachers and enable schools to emphasise the part that personal and social development plays in what they can offer children and young people.

Staff who reflect the local community

With a relatively short but effective induction and training, learning mentors in particular are likely to be recruited from the community around the school. They have often worked for the school before becoming a learning mentor, for instance as a teaching assistant or school secretary. They may be younger than teachers and can be role models for children and young people, sometimes representing groups not usually found in the teaching profession such as young black men. The fact that they are more representative of the local community can also help break down barriers with parents.

They [learning mentors] often come from the similar backgrounds to the pupils they work with and know the difficulties they face (Ofsted 2003a).
Ofsted

Learning mentors can be closer to our age group sometimes.
YP seminar

Enthusiasm and innovation

Overwhelmingly, the PAs and learning mentors we talked to for this project were enthusiastic about their role and excited to be part of an emerging new profession. This enthusiasm has an impact on the lengths to which they will go to get things right for the children and young people with whom they work. The examples of good practice in Section 4 are ample demonstration of this.

With this wealth of skills, knowledge and positive attitudes it is hardly surprising that a learning mentor said: 'One parent wanted to know why her child hadn't got a learning mentor.'

3 What schools can do to make the best use of support staff

Introducing new staff roles into an organisation such as a school will inevitably bring about a change in relationships and a need to restructure existing systems. With the move to an extended workforce for children and young people in schools, it is important to take stock of what can be learned from bringing in Connexions PAs and learning mentors, to identify the factors that help and those that hinder.

This section summarises the key points made by support staff, teachers and senior management teams we talked to in the course of this project.

What helps?

A well-written contract or agreement

Most schools we talked to benefit from a partnership agreement with the local Connexions Service or Excellence in Cities Partnership. The agreements outlined clearly the level of service and the range of activities being supported.

A positive attitude to pastoral support and PSHE

Schools that give a high priority to pastoral support and understand the importance of children and young people's personal and social development in enabling them to achieve, are more likely to make effective use of support staff and see them as crucial partners in raising standards.

The main barriers to good PSHE and Citizenship are the teachers and the classroom environment.
Connexions PA, community college

An inclusive school culture

Schools that work to ensure that all children and young people achieve and flourish value the different members of the school community.

A supportive senior management team

All support staff we talked to emphasised the importance of the senior management team understanding their role and publicly supporting their work to staff, pupils and parents.

Integration of support staff into the whole-school team

Learning mentors and Connexions staff stressed that to work effectively it was essential that they are seen as an integral part of the whole-school team. In practice, this means making sure that support staff are included in staff meetings, are welcome in the staff room and included in social events.

The senior management team are just beginning to use the term 'staff' in their memos instead of 'teachers'.
Learning mentor, primary school

Good communication

Support staff need to be included in communications, both within the school and from the LEA and other organisations. It is also helpful if support staff are able to feed back the range of issues that children and young people are facing anonymously so the whole staff team develops a positive awareness of the range of issues facing children and young people.

A clear referral system backed by regular meetings

With a growing number of support staff working in schools, it is vital to have a clear referral process which involves all key staff. Schools that have set up regular meetings to bring all such staff together, including those who come in from other agencies, have found this an ideal way to share information and avoid duplication.

Where it works well, schools have some sort of forum to bring together all the agencies working in the school.
Connexions manager

Having good links with other staff and agencies through the referral group has been a huge help.
Connexions PA

One key person chosen to liaise within the school

Although it is vital that support staff link up with each other, they emphasised the need for one key member of staff – who has good communication with other key people – to take responsibility for their work and sort out problems. Usually this will be a member of the senior management team.

Opportunities to work with all the school's children and young people

Many of the PAs and learning mentors we talked to saw the opportunity to work with a wider range of children and young people in the school as a positive strategy for enabling them to see their targeted pupils in their normal context. It also helped to get their faces known in the school, and destigmatised seeking help. Out-of-school activities and contributions to PSHE and Citizenship are good opportunities for wider work. See Section 4 for more details.

A suitable space

Support staff need appropriate space within the school to work with children and young people on a one-to-one basis as well as group sessions and drop-in facilities. In many of the schools visited, support staff have created areas with informal seating and colourful decor so that pupils feel comfortable and welcome. This has had a positive impact on the way that children and young people perceive the support provision.

LEA-level, multi-agency training on PSHE and Citizenship issues

Learning mentors and PAs spoke positively about opportunities to attend training courses with teachers and workers from local agencies on a range of themes, which enabled them to make contacts and learn about local agendas.

What hinders?

Lack of clarity about roles

The flipside of the flexibility of PAs' and learning mentors' roles is a lack of clarity which sometimes means that they are used inappropriately (for example, driving a minibus or minding a class). Although these support workers are willing to become involved in a wide range of activities, there must be clear boundaries about what is appropriate and effective in removing barriers to learning.

I would say that the PA role is not yet clearly understood especially by ordinary classroom teachers. When I was a teacher, I wouldn't have seen the importance of it.
Connexions PA, community college

Part-time support staff not feeling part of the school

Support workers who are attached to more than one school, and who may not be employed by the school, can experience difficulties in becoming an established member of the school with the result that neither teachers nor pupils understand their role.

Resistance from some managers and teachers

Negative attitudes to the role of support staff were shown by some headteachers, senior management team members and class teachers. These can cause difficulties for support staff in 'breaking into' the group of teaching staff to explain their role and communicate with them about individuals and groups with whom they are working.

Initially, teachers did not see [learning mentors] as being professionals. We had to work hard to build up a good relationship with the teachers.
Learning mentor, community college

There was some resentment of the [learning mentors] at first, especially when we observed children in class. But now the teachers can see how the children we work with have benefited and they come to us and ask for support.
Learning mentor, primary school

Inflexible timetable arrangements

In most schools, support staff are careful not to withdraw children and young people from the same lesson each week, and there are clear systems which teachers understand. In others, inflexible planning means that it is difficult to get pupils out of lessons for one-to-one or group work.

Referrals channelled through one person

In some schools referrals for support have to be channelled through just one person, for example, the deputy head or the designated 'link learning mentor'. This can create a lack of shared understanding of the needs of individual young people and may result in a young person not accessing the right form of support and create a 'bottle neck' in the system which may slow down effective referrals.

Lack of clarity about who works with whom

Different support workers may be tasked with working with different groups of pupils, and there may be a lack of clarity about transitions from one service to another. With learning mentors and Connexions PAs, for example, schools may need to plan a 'handover' of pupils at Key Stage 4, as Connexions only works with 14- to 19-year-olds.

Support staff not included in LEA communications

Advisory staff, special education needs teams and other LEA staff are not always aware of the role of support staff such as PAs and learning mentors, and do not always send information about PSHE and Citizenship and pastoral issues to them.

Differences in pay, career structure and qualifications

At present, the many different support workers in schools come from a range of backgrounds and organisations. A culture of professionalism which values all support staff, and a focus on the needs of children and young people, will minimise resentment between different professional groups.

In summary, the factors that support staff, teachers and senior management teams cited as helpful when bringing in Connexions PAs and learning mentors are:

- a well-written contract or agreement with the school
- a positive attitude by the school to pastoral support and personal and social development
- a culture in the school that supports inclusion
- a supportive senior management team
- the integration of support staff into a whole-school team
- good communication at all levels
- regular meetings for all support staff in schools and a clear referral system
- one key person chosen to liaise within the school
- opportunities to work with all the children and young people in the school
- a suitable space
- multi-agency training on PSHE and Citizenship issues at LEA level.

The factors they cited as likely to hinder are:

- lack of clarity about roles
- part-time support staff not feeling part of the school
- resistance from some headteachers, senior management and teachers
- inflexible timetable arrangements
- referrals channelled through only one person
- lack of clarity about who works with who
- support staff not included in LEA communications
- differences in pay, career structure and qualifications.

4 Examples of good practice

Examples of good practice are presented here under the following categories:

- Coordinated approaches
- PSHE and Citizenship in the curriculum
- Work on specific health issues
- Transitions
- Out-of-school activities
- Empowerment and participation
- Working with parents and carers
- Drop-in services

Coordinated approaches

Collaborative working between learning mentors, Connexions PAs and other support staff is strongly recommended in much of the key documentation and DfES guidance. The main vehicle for collaboration is a forum which regularly brings together all relevant parties with key school staff and managers. These groups go by a variety of names: social inclusion team; guidance forum or network; pastoral support team; and student guidance and support team. Key issues for the group to discuss include: identifying the needs of learners; setting up coherent recording and referral systems; monitoring practice; confidentiality;

communication between support and teaching staff; integrating support and guidance within the school ethos; and the structures and systems of the school as a whole. In primary schools, the smaller number of pupils and staff mean that arrangements can be more informal. Secondary schools have tackled this in a variety of ways – discussed in the following case studies.

Case study one: Referral group at Sydney Stringer School and Community Technology College

At Sydney Stringer School and Community Technology College in Coventry there is a referral group, which meets weekly, and is attended by the manager of learning support, two assistant headteachers responsible for inclusion and the lower school, the head of social inclusion, the education welfare officer, the lead learning mentor, the Connexions PA and learning support staff. The group deals with students from Key Stages 3 and 4 on alternate weeks. Referrals come from form tutors, via the heads of years and assistant heads. In this school, the learning mentors work with Key Stage 3 students then, at Key Stage 4, Connexions PAs take over with a special emphasis on considering alternative curricular provision. Learning mentors and Connexions staff take part in the system of yellow 'good news/bad news' slips on an equal basis with teaching staff. Connexions work is divided between two PAs: one who concentrates on careers education and guidance and one who provides more intensive support. They say:

I can help pupils see the bigger picture and enable them to think about where they're going.

I can take young people's agenda to the school and advocate for them.

Learning mentors provide one-to-one sessions and run a number of groups including 'It's good to be me' at which students are only allowed to say positive things. They also run buddy groups for Years 7 and 8 pupils. They have introduced and facilitated the DfES Thinking Challenge Project for all pupils in Year 8, bringing together groups of pupils from different tutor groups. They say:

We can help pupils see things from the teachers' perspective and recognise the realities of school.

Case study two: Learning mentors and Connexions PAs at Greenford High School, Ealing

The lead learning mentor at this school for 11- to 18-year-olds in west London was appointed head of social inclusion in 2001, and manages a team of staff including the full-time learning mentor, the pastoral support worker, two teaching assistants, the school nurse/welfare officer, two part-time Connexions PAs and the school counsellor. She also coordinates the work undertaken by external mentors and works closely with the study centre (Ealing's pupil referral unit). She is also the Healthy Schools coordinator. Most members of the team are based in the 'Purple Room', furnished with easy chairs and cushions where pupils can drop in and know they can find someone to talk to.

The work of social inclusion is underpinned by the work of other teams such as the pastoral team (heads of house, Key Stages 3 and 4 coordinators, deputy head and special educational needs coordinator), the school welfare service and form tutors. There are well-developed systems for behaviour interventions, including the 'traffic lights' system (which alerts pupils, parents, staff and the LEA about concern levels relating to a pupil's behaviour, as well as learning mentors and the peer-assisted learning scheme (PALS). PALS involves Year 12 students in mentoring students in Years 9 and 10. PALS mentors receive two days' training and are supervised by school staff. The school also has a well-planned system of referral routes, managed by the lead learning mentor/head of social inclusion, with a series of regular meetings to support the process.

The Connexions PA is based in an accessible, attractively refurbished office which also serves as the Careers Library. She aims to see all Year 11 students and all students in Year 9 who are on the special educational needs (SEN) register. She routinely goes into PSHE and Citizenship lessons in Years 9, 10 and 11 to introduce Connexions, talk about choosing options and start vocational assessments. This is followed up with small group sessions on issues such as modern apprenticeships. She works closely with the learning mentors who will bring students to see her where necessary and can refer students on to one of the 25 intensive PAs in Ealing. She says:

What I value most is the opportunity to share information with the rest of the social inclusion team. It helps me to know about family problems the students may be dealing with.

Student A referred himself to the learning mentors because he had heard that they were OK from other students and wanted help with anger and frustration. He has had access to one-to-one sessions and group work with the learning mentor. The use of role play has helped him deal with situations he finds hard to manage with teachers and other pupils. He has also worked with his learning mentor with the Kar2ouche[1] computer program which allows students to create their own scenarios and outcomes. A meeting was arranged for him with the Connexions PA which 'helped me look into what I'm going to be doing in future' and gave him information about colleges, universities and courses. He commented,

I would probably have been kicked out for fighting and anger problems. Learning mentors are not like teachers, you can talk to them more like friends, it's more confidential and relaxed, you can have jokes with them.

Student B was referred to a learning mentor because she was often involved in arguments with other students – 'I'm the loud one and I get in trouble'. She has found the one-to-one and group work role play sessions really practical in helping her to develop new skills to deal with these situations. She couldn't believe how effective the strategies she had learnt were in dealing with teachers and suspected the learning mentor had told the teacher to act differently – 'It really works. He [the learning mentor] taught me that if you show respect, you'll be respected back.'

---

1   This is developed by Immersive Education www.immersiveeducation.com/uk

Case study three: Connexions PA at Girls' Grammar School, Torquay

At Torquay Girls' Grammar School, the Connexions PA was the school's original careers advisor. She has developed this role to incorporate more intensive aspects of the PA's role. She sees the two aspects of her job as complementary rather than in opposition. The universal careers role ensures that she is known throughout the school and removes stigma for students going to see her on an individual basis. She attends head of year and form tutor meetings, and also frequently drops into the staff room. There is a clear communication process for referrals through the head, year heads and form tutors, and students can also self-refer by discreetly putting a note in a contact box.

Although the school serves a prosperous, middle-class area and selects its intake, the pupils have complex choices to make and often need support to deal with parental pressure. The PA also sees students with a range of typical adolescent problems, which do not disappear just because they are bright. They have included home and family problems where relationships have broken down, sexual orientation, drug and alcohol issues, self-harm and relationships with peers.

At LEA level, learning mentors and Connexions PAs are working with PSHE and Citizenship advisors and Healthy School coordinators to integrate curricular approaches, organise joint training and share good practice.

Other examples

In Greater Merseyside, the Connexions Partnership has worked with the University of Liverpool to map PSHE practice across the city and to produce *Actively Making Connections Work*, a good practice guide to multidisciplinary working for learning mentors and PAs in the secondary school sector. This identifies how schools can set up multidisciplinary 'guidance communities' and gives a number of useful case studies at school and LEA level.

In Knowsley, part of Greater Merseyside, the PSHE advisor and the Connexions curriculum advisor attend each others' coordinators' meetings and have worked together to update the LEA's PSHE guidance. They have also established a good working relationship with the Healthy Schools team and the Excellence in Cities learning mentors team. Similarly, in Leicester, the Connexions curriculum development team has produced *Preparing Students for their Learning and Working Life*, an integrated careers education, Citizenship and PSHE resource for Key Stages 3 and 4.

Together, the Coventry Excellence Cluster and the Connexions service have directly addressed the question of collaborative working by producing *Good Practice Draft Guidance for Personal Advisors and Learning Mentors – Emerging practice to develop effective working arrangements in schools* (2004). This guidance defines activities that could be undertaken jointly by Connexions PAs and learning mentors, such as joint home visits and drop-in clinics, as well as those which are complementary, such as taking part in school inclusion teams.

In Cambridgeshire, the PSHE advisor, in liaison with a multidisciplinary steering group, has developed a county-wide personal development programme which allows people and organisations who support schools to see where their contribution fits in.

In many areas, such as Blackburn and Bradford, joint training events involving learning mentors, Connexions PAs, Healthy Schools coordinators, PSHE and Citizenship advisors, teachers, and even in some cases primary care trust staff, have attempted to make classroom practice consistent, particularly in the fields of drug education and sex and relationships education, and to develop a multi-agency working ethos within the area.

PSHE and Citizenship in the curriculum

Although there is a debate about how much time support staff should spend in the classroom, Connexions PAs and learning mentors are contributing to the taught PSHE and Citizenship curriculum in a number of ways. Working with children and young people across the school, as well as with targeted individuals, provides an opportunity to see pupils in a normal context and helps staff to see how their work fits in with a very relevant part of the curriculum.

Most learning mentors and PAs in secondary schools take time to visit PSHE and Citizenship lessons and tutor groups, especially in Year 7, to introduce themselves and remind young people about how they can help. At Richard Lander School in Truro, these sessions are now built into the pupil development scheme of work. Some secondary school learning mentors have been instrumental in supporting the introduction of circle time in tutor time. They can also provide input on specific curriculum projects: such as in an Enfield school, where learning mentors liaised with the head of History to work on Black History Month; or at Grange Technology College in Bradford, where the learning mentors have been involved in supporting young people in the annual Magistrates Court competition.

Both learning mentors and Connexions PAs often contribute to curriculum enrichment days on a range of issues from drug education to the Real Game (see page 37). Connexions PAs contribute especially to careers education and guidance, particularly that relating to work experience. Sometimes they take a creative approach, such as the secondary school where the PA devised a series of practical tasks such as dismantling and reassembling a carburettor to encourage students to explore their personal competencies. Support workers are also well placed to make links with local organisations who can come in and contribute to PSHE and Citizenship.

Learning mentors and Connexions PAs are also involved in schemes to accredit PSHE and Citizenship. In Birmingham, they are part of a multi-agency team which is piloting an Award for Citizenship. On the Isle of Wight, Connexions runs Chrysalis Compact Clubs for disaffected young people who have to complete six personally devised challenges to achieve the award. So far, these have included learning to drive a tractor, tidying their bedroom and writing a story.

Case study four: The work of the learning mentor at the Ravenscroft School

The learning mentor at this secondary school in Barnet works to promote students' personal, social and emotional development across the school. In routine one-to-one and group sessions she has focused on issues such as self-esteem, conflict resolution, anger management and empowerment. She has also contributed to two PSHE and Citizenship off-timetable days for Year 7, liaising with the year coordinator to run circle-time sessions and group discussions on drugs and peer pressure. In her room, information books are available for students on topics such as sexually transmitted infections (STIs), drugs, growing up, smoking and bereavement. She runs regular drop-in sessions at break-times and a friendship club at lunchtimes, and has helped set up a peer listening scheme as part of the school's anti-bullying strategy. She also regularly takes part in home visits to students and their families to encourage school refusers back to school and to tackle truancy.

Case study five: Learning mentors at Laisterdyke High School

The assistant head (support and guidance), who is also the PSHE coordinator, manages the learning mentors at this mixed secondary school in Bradford. Learning mentors are attached to a particular year group and attend year group meetings. Referrals are made through the year leader, and students can also refer themselves. As well as running one-to-one sessions, the learning mentors coordinate lots of different groups, for example a low ability nurture group in Year 9, a Year 7 transition group, and after-school and lunchtime groups including the homework group, a cycling proficiency club, aromatherapy sessions and a body image and confidence course, run jointly with the youth service. Through their line manager, the learning mentors are also involved with a number of PSHE curriculum projects, such as the Things We Don't Talk About project on issues to do with sexual exploitation which is being run jointly with the Barnardo's Streets and Lanes Project. The Year 11 learning mentor sits in on SRE lessons to follow up on any concerns. Learning mentors support their year group on off-timetable days, such as the Critical Skills Community Day which culminated in a 'full-service' contract for students setting out the support and advice that they are entitled to through the school.

The learning mentors are now fully accepted and valued across the school, although there were some initial concerns from teachers who were worried that they were being observed and judged.

Case study six: Connexions and the Real Game at Kesteven and Sleaford Grammar School, Lincolnshire

Connexions has made an obvious difference to Kesteven and Sleaford Grammar School in terms of providing access to high-quality information and advice about future choices and careers. The Connexions PA also uses the Real Game, a careers education simulation designed to help pupils in Years 8 and 9 explore the world of work in an enjoyable and relevant way. There are obvious links with PSHE and Citizenship. Developed originally in Canada, it has been adapted for use in the UK where it is promoted and funded through Connexions Partnerships, which provide training and support for teachers on how to run the game. There are also versions for Years 6 and 7 (Make It Real) and for Years 10 and 11 (Be Real).

During one session with Year 8 groups, pupils start by creating their own 'dream cloud' – a wish list of the kind of housing, transport, possessions and leisure activities that they aspire to as an adult. Most opt for a five-bedroom house with swimming pool and a sports car. Reality kicks in when they are (randomly) allocated a job with appropriate qualifications and salary. They then have to start budgeting for living expenses and some choose to substitute more realistic choices, such as swapping the sports car for a bike. Students then have to budget their time and work out how much is left for leisure activities. Chance cards are dealt out at intervals bringing unexpected bonuses (for instance, finding £50 while tidying the house) or setbacks (having to spend £75 on a pair of glasses). They work in groups to choose a holiday which everyone in the group can afford. Interspersed throughout are 'spin game' quizzes which test students' knowledge of skills and qualifications needed for different jobs, and attitudes about gender stereotyping.

The students clearly enjoyed the session and immediately engaged with the scenarios. There was much swapping of opinions and feelings, likes and dislikes as they discussed the relative merits of certain lifestyle choices. Students appreciated the different way of learning offered by the game. As one girl said:

It's not like other lessons where we just sit and listen. With this, we get to think for ourselves and work things out for ourselves.

Work on specific health issues

Learning mentors and Connexions staff are in an ideal position to contribute to a number of national public health priorities including mental health, teenage pregnancy and drug education. As the examples below show, they are finding interesting and sometimes innovative ways to do this.

Emotional health and well-being

Emotional problems can seriously interfere with children and young people's ability to learn and take part at school. Learning mentors in many areas have had specific training on emotional health. For example, in Camden they have received training on solution-focused thinking and emotional literacy. They are able to put the knowledge and skills that they have acquired into both one-to-one and group work sessions, focusing on self-esteem, stress management, anger management and bereavement. Learning mentors in an Enfield school have organised a girls' self-esteem group that included a visit to the local FE college for a full makeover and hair design. In one school in Hillingdon, learning mentors run meditation sessions. Learning mentors in Lambeth and Waltham Forest are working with teaching staff to introduce the Second Step Programme, an award-winning curriculum programme designed to teach children to recognise and understand feelings, make positive and effective choices and keep anger from escalating into violence. At Copland Community School in Wembley, learning mentors have developed group work programmes for young women and young men, looking at peer pressure, gender roles, parenthood, influences and healthy eating.

Sexual health and teenage pregnancy

Part of the role of both learning mentors and Connexions PAs is to make links with organisations in the local community. Through sex and relationships education (SRE) they identify useful professionals to support the PSHE curriculum and pupils' health and welfare. Connexions staff in some areas have taken an active part in multi-agency sexual health roadshows aimed at educating young people about contraception, sexual health services and other issues. Their reports show that they are often also involved in the local teenage pregnancy implementation group which teaching staff would find difficult to attend.

Although learning mentors are less involved in teenage pregnancy prevention, they carry out other important work relating to sexual health. At one primary school, the learning mentor works alongside the class teachers in the SRE programme to provide a male role model and to work with groups of boys. The learning mentors at Laisterdyke High School in Bradford often arrange to sit in on SRE lessons with Year 11, so that they can pick up on any issues that arise. They also work with pregnant schoolgirls and mothers under 16 at the maternity unit each week.

Alcohol and other drugs

Like many PSHE and Citizenship issues, drugs can fundamentally affect children and young people's personal lives, and so can create barriers to learning. By being aware of what is happening in PSHE lessons, learning mentors are often able to use their expertise and skills to support the teacher. In one school in Enfield, learning mentors have worked with teachers and the police to organise a debate on drugs and the law. In another Enfield school, smoking groups have been set up, usually where students have been caught smoking. Rather than using a purely disciplinary approach, learning mentors help students to discuss ways of giving up and of supporting each other, so turning it into a positive learning experience. Connexions PAs and learning mentors in Blackburn have received training in harm-reduction approaches so as to target work with young drug users in schools.

Some learning mentors and PAs have been trained to work on a one-to-one basis with young people with drug problems. As with SRE, learning mentors and Connexions PAs are well placed to link up with local services, including the school nurse.

Transitions

Transitions from one phase of education to the next can be particularly difficult for vulnerable young people. Support staff, such as Connexions PAs and learning mentors, play a vital role in providing targeted support at these times.

Connexions PAs have carried out valuable work on the transition to Key Stage 4 and also on the transition to work, further education or training. As part of this work, they also contribute to Careers Education and Guidance in Years 10 and 11 and advise on work experience and alternative education programmes. They also have a specific remit to work with all Year 9 students with special educational needs as they select their options and enter Year 10. They can continue to work with vulnerable young people after they have left school, as they go to college or into work.

For learning mentors, the transition from primary to secondary school is often the main focus. Some are designated to work specifically on transition issues. Learning mentors in Camden have developed their own transition programme. Class teachers and form tutors in Years 6 and 7 are trained to deliver a series of eight workshops addressing issues affecting children transferring to secondary school.

In many areas, primary and secondary learning mentors liaise with each other to ensure that information about particularly vulnerable pupils is shared. In Bradford, Network Transition Days bring learning mentors from both phases together to discuss issues and share good practice. At Copland Community School in Wembley, learning mentors run the Transition Mentoring Project which involves groups of Year 7 students visiting primary schools and then being around on the first day of the September term to welcome the new Year 7 students. At Ravenscroft High School in Barnet, the learning mentor runs a friendship club for Years 7 and 8. At a school in Enfield, the learning mentor works with the SENCO to identify pupils who need extra help as they arrive at the school. Weekly meetings take place at which they discuss scenarios, play team and friendship games and encourage the pupils to participate in extra-curricular activities. Learning mentors have also been involved in a 'taster' day for Year 6 pupils at which they have introduced themselves to the pupils. In some schools, learning mentors are attached to particular year groups. This helps to build up the knowledge and trust of pupils.

Out-of-school activities

A key benefit of support staff such as Connexions PAs and learning mentors is that they can work with children and young people outside and beyond the school day, particularly on projects which focus on personal development. The funding that has been available to support these projects has enabled a wide variety of activities to take place. Learning mentors in particular organise clubs and other activities at breakfast, lunchtime and after school. Often these are open to all pupils at the school, not just those referred for support. Some Connexions Partnerships are the lead agency and others provide support for the government's Positive Activities for Young People (PAYP), a major programme of holiday activities for vulnerable young people (see the Connexions Leicestershire case study for further details).

Clubs run by learning mentors are immensely varied and in some cases unusual, often reflecting their previous skills and experiences. Many learning mentors use their knowledge of the local area to find tutors to run sessions popular with young people. In Bradford, a learning mentor asked the boys in one school what sort of after-school club they would be interested in, after noticing that few were attending. He found a tutor to run a breakdancing club for older boys who then helped to pass on the skills to younger pupils.

Other, less obvious, out-of-school clubs around the country include an aromatherapy club, a puzzle club, a Warhammer (role-playing battle game) club, a comic club, an Italian language group, cycling proficiency, a Christian group, a body image club, a DJ/MC club. At Grange Technology College in Bradford, the Grange Girls' Nature Club is run in association with the Countryside Service. At one school in Enfield, a quiet activities club, featuring art, drama, reading and puppets, caters for the needs of children who have difficulties relating to their peers. It also acts as a friendship group for those with low self-esteem. Amongst the majority of schools, sports, art and craft activities and homework clubs form the basis of most provision.

Both Connexions staff and learning mentors are often involved in organising residential activities and other trips and visits for young people, as they may have more time and fewer curriculum commitments than teachers. The learning mentor from John Kelly Girls School, for example, was able to bring a group of students to the consultation seminar which informed this book. The learning mentor at Copland Community School organises an annual residential trip to the Forest of Dean to develop independence, self-confidence and problem-solving skills. She has also organised a project jointly with the Tricycle Theatre in Kilburn during which students wrote, performed and produced their own play, taking full responsibility for everything including stage management and props. One learning mentor arranged a team building and self-esteem raising event for local young people with help from Spurs Football Club. Learning mentors will also often arrange shorter trips as a reward for those of the mentored children and young people who have made progress in meeting their agreed targets. This might include visits to football matches, ice skating or bowling.

The RAGS Project

Connexions Tees Valley has supported a project in Redcar which encourages young people to try out work-related activities which are not gender stereotypical. RAGS (Redcar Against Gender Stereotyping) took place during school hours, at weekends and during school holidays. Activities included a young firefighters' group for girls that was set up in association with Cleveland Fire Brigade. One girl commented:

It has been great because if there had been boys there, we would not have felt as confident. When we did the ladder training, if one of us was nervous we were there to support them. If there had been boys there, they would have laughed at us.

There were also an accredited e-media course with Redcar and Cleveland College, and carousel events for Years 7 and 8 with Equality North-East. The project was guided by two focus groups, one consisting of key partners in the Redcar area such as training providers, employers, youth inclusion and the Early Years Partnership, and the other consisting of young people in Years 7 to 11 from three schools. There are now plans for a childcare course for boys.

Connexions Leicestershire: Positive Activities for Young People and the U Project

Launched in July 2003, Positive Activities for Young People (PAYP) is a new national scheme of developmental activities for young people at risk. The aim of the programme is to reduce youth offending and to encourage and support young people in returning to education or training. Building on the success of earlier 'Splash' programmes and the Connexions Summer Plus schemes, it is funded by the New Opportunities Fund (NOF), the DfES and the Home Office, initially for three years. The programme's emphasis is on providing quality sports, arts and creative activities that are not only appealing but also focus on each young person's individual needs, equipping them with new skills, improving their self-esteem and breaking down ethnic and cultural barriers. Key worker support – provided through the Connexions Service – helps those most at risk.

In Leicestershire, the Connexions service is the lead development agency for PAYP and has ensured that the provision is led by the expressed needs of local 8- to 14-year-olds. Vulnerable young people are specially targeted and are referred by PAs in, for example, Youth Offending Team and Social Services. Activities include sports, street dancing, DJ workshops, song writing and video production. PAYP Leicestershire also aims to create activities in areas where there is nothing going on. The starting point may be events such as sports activities or street dance in a local park or leisure centre. This was so successful on one occasion that whole families came out with picnics and bottles of wine for staff.

The U Project (**U**nlimited, **U**nmissable, **U**nbelievable, **U**nexpected) is a national programme for vulnerable students who leave full-time education at 16 with no plans for what to do next. Funded by the NOF, it is a personal development programme offering structured activities and support with the aim of helping students to make positive choices. Participants get together regularly in a group between Easter and the summer facilitated by a group worker, with participants being given one-to-one support from a Connexions PA. In 2003, Leicestershire hosted 30 projects with activities ranging from motorbike maintenance and a Caribbean Carnival, to sports and music. The aim was to encourage confidence, communication and the skills of teamwork as well as possibly leading to a vocational qualification or a desire to return to education. Many projects culminated in a residential experience, for example, a theatre skills trip to the Edinburgh Festival and a 'Girls' Breakout' residential trip for pregnant teenage girls. The programme ended with a celebration event at the Y Theatre to showcase young people's new skills and recognise their achievements. One girl who attended the residential at the Edinburgh Festival said:

By the end of the course I was so happy, because I felt I had done an amazing job. I had learned a lot, I got the experience of being away from home, working for the first time, I learned some cooking from other people I shared a flat with.

Empowerment and participation

The introduction of Connexions PAs and learning mentors has helped to support children and young people's participation at LEA and school level.

Most Connexions Partnerships have a designated member of staff with responsibility for youth empowerment or participation at an LEA or partnership level. In Merton Connexions in South London, the participation officer helps to coordinate the Youth Forum, and to organise representatives from schools and youth settings, as well as helping them to arrange an annual youth conference. She also coordinates the participation of schools in the national Youth Parliament, organising the selection of candidates and voting procedures across all the secondary schools in the borough.

Learning mentors are more likely to be involved in developing children and young people's participation at school level. They may be involved in supporting the school council or in setting up and supporting a range of peer mentoring schemes. These could be simple buddy schemes, particularly for Years 7 and 8, or a graduate mentoring scheme in which mentors accompany their mentees to colleges and universities. An example of a fully developed peer mentoring scheme supported by the LEA, and with training for mentors, is the scheme run at Highams Park School, Waltham Forest, North London.

Encouraging young people in Leicester to participate

In Leicester, the youth involvement officer encourages young people to participate in a number of ways. Staff recruitment and selection is an area where they play a key role. Drawn from the ranks of those not in education, employment and training, so that there is no problem with attending interviews during the day, they go through six to eight hours of accredited training before they can short-list and interview. The young interviewers create their own questions and tasks.

The youth involvement officer has also brought together groups of young people to participate in consultations and surveys, such as *Every Child Matters* and the regional sports strategy. She has worked hard to develop the Youth Executive which now includes young mothers, young people in care and non-school attenders. PAs across the city often refer young people to her to get them involved in participation projects. As in many other areas, young people are encouraged to attend the Connexions Local Management Committee. In Leicester, this process has been made easier and more attractive to young people by arranging the meeting at cabaret style tables, having name badges and a system of green and red cards to show if you want to speak (green) or if you don't understand (red). These are used by adults as well. The only disadvantage of having a dedicated officer for participation is that other officers may think that they do not have to tackle this issue.

Peer mentoring at Highams Park School, Waltham Forest

The school – a voluntary aided technology college – has a learning mentor who is also head of sixth form and head of careers. The peer mentoring scheme has been in place for two years, after the learning mentors in Waltham Forest attended a training course on running the scheme. This means that they can now provide a two-day training course for students which is accredited by the Open College Network.

To become a peer mentor, students have to apply formally with a reference and be interviewed. The main focus of the mentoring is Year 7, and mentors accompany the head of Year 7 to visit local primary schools. Peer mentors are also attached to a particular tutor group and spend about 20 minutes in the mornings with their tutor group once or twice a week. They help their mentees with reading, keeping their school planners up-to-date, finishing homework, setting targets and getting their equipment organised. Some also go to PSHE lessons and support their mentees there. They also help to staff the drop-in clinic in the learning mentor area, which is brightly painted and comfortably furnished. The most common problems that they deal with include missing lessons, bullying, causing trouble, bereavement and family illness. The peer mentors meet, all together, every half term and know that they can turn to the learning mentor for advice and support. Reflecting on the experience, one peer mentor said, 'It's good knowing that you're helping and making a difference. You see them go from being very quiet and shy to being very bouncy with more friends.' Another one added, 'You get a lot more confident as you go on. It has made me much more confident seeing my mentee becoming more willing to talk to me.' All appreciated the opportunity to attend the Waltham Forest peer mentoring conference organised by the learning mentor coordinator.

Working with parents and carers

Working with parents and carers is a crucial area for support workers, and many of those we spoke to are involved in home visits or working with families and care staff in the school. This is often to do with the transitions, either into primary school, up to secondary school, or into work or further education.

Being able to understand the home circumstances of children and young people and to relate that to their behaviour at school was seen as central to the work of support staff by those taking part in the project. Learning mentors at Lidget Green Primary School have developed a very pro-active approach to involving families.

Learning mentors at Lidget Green Primary School, Bradford

The two full-time learning mentors have been in post since 2001 and are involved in a range of activities to create an inclusive school, including one-to-one sessions for pupils referred by class teachers, targeted groups on issues such as self-esteem and bullying, after-school clubs and events.

A major focus of their work has been to find creative ways of involving parents in the life and work of the school. The most successful and popular event has been a Pop Idol contest for which 130 children auditioned to be chosen for one of only 10 acts. They borrowed a stage from the local secondary school and the school secretary's husband provided lights. A learning mentor at the school noted

The event did so much for children's self-esteem and it brought parents in who had never been in to the school before.

Another popular event that attracted parents and carers was an Easter Egg Hunt in which teams had to crack a code to find the prize. Organising such events can take effort, but the results are worth it, as one learning mentor explained:

Organising these events is time consuming, but everyone is agreed that the impact on parental involvement is worth it – more parents than ever before were involved in the school fair last year.

The learning mentors have also been actively supporting a Family Friends project, a seven-week parenting course. The learning mentors helped to recruit parents and to follow up the course with further referrals and by organising on-going groups.

Drop-in services

Connexions PAs, learning mentors and other support staff are often involved in setting up and running drop-in advice sessions for children and young people both in and out of school. The Connexions service in most areas has set up a 'one-stop shop'. Typically situated in a high street or other conspicuous area, as in Merton and Leicester, these are run in partnership with a number of other local agencies such as alcohol and drugs services, sexual health and family planning services, and youth services. Learning mentors in Bradford can refer young people to TIC TAC (Teenage Information Centre Teenage Advice Centre) centres in two schools where young people can access information, support and advice on a range of health and other issues from a multidisciplinary team. In Blackburn, Connexions are providing a PA for a TIC TAC Centre.

5 Key messages for schools

The following are some of the key messages drawn from the project's findings.

- Support staff such as learning mentors and Connexions PAs bring a new professional dimension into school and play a key role in inclusion and addressing inequalities.
- Personal, social and emotional development is at the heart of raising education standards and support staff have a key role to play in this aspect of education.
- Many children and young people need access to well-planned opportunities for personal, social and emotional development and support and advice at school if they are to achieve.
- Consistent backing from the school's senior management team is crucial if support staff are to make an impact on raising education standards.
- Support staff need to be integrated into the whole staff team as part of a whole-school approach to personal and social development.
- All school staff need to be aware of the roles of support workers, such as learning mentors and Connexions PAs, and should help to promote their work to children and young people.
- A system needs to be set up to enable ongoing communication and information sharing between support staff and teaching staff.
- Children and young people will become familiar with the work of support staff, and seeking help will be destigmatised, if their

presence is visible and active throughout the whole school and not just targeted at vulnerable pupils.
- A structure to coordinate the work of support staff from different agencies will need to be planned and managed by a senior member of staff.
- Support staff bring a range of strengths and skills and allow creative approaches to personal and social development across the school.
- Support staff may be used flexibly, but a clear agreement about their role will prevent them being used inappropriately.
- A dedicated and appropriate space with adequate privacy for support staff will enhance the quality of their work with individuals and help make their presence felt in the school.

Connexions PAs and learning mentors have developed new ways of providing support for vulnerable pupils through personal, social and emotional development in a remarkably short space of time. Their role has been welcomed and acknowledged by headteachers, teachers, Ofsted and, most importantly, children and young people.

The examples of good practice highlighted in this book show the range and breadth of their work, much of which has brought new insights into what works for vulnerable children.

In general, schools have been quick to make use of the added skills and experience that these support roles bring in helping to meet the needs of children whom they have found hard to engage in learning. Many schools now find it difficult to imagine how they would do without them.

Headteachers say that if they had to make cuts, learning mentors would be the last to go.
Learning mentor coordinator, Leicester

As we move into an era of extended schools and an extended school workforce, it will be important to get the balance right between the role of teaching staff and that of support staff. Children and young people will not benefit if teachers have no further responsibility for personal, social and emotional development and simply shift all such work onto support staff. New relationships and structures will need to be formed to bridge the work of different professional groups. This will create a whole-school approach in which teaching and learning, support and advice work hand in hand to provide a seamless experience for children and young people, enabling them to succeed as learners and as human beings.

The learning that has been gained from the work of learning mentors and Connexions PAs is extremely useful in thinking about how support services, provided by a range of professionals for children and young people in schools, can best be developed in future.

References and further reading

Calouste Gulbenkian Foundation (1998) *Learning by Heart: The role of emotional education in raising school achievement.* London: Calouste Gulbenkian Foundation.

Connexions Leicestershire (2003), *Preparing Students for Their Learning and Working Life: An integrated careers education, citizenship and PSHE resource for Key Stages 3 and 4.* Leicester: Connexions Leicestershire.

Connexions Service National Unit (2003) *Building Connexions: Information and guidance for integrating Connexions into schools.* Sheffield: Department for Education and Skills.

Coventry Excellence Cluster and Connexions Service (2004) *Good Practice Draft Guidance for Personal Advisors and Learning Mentors.* Coventry: Connexions Coventry and Warwickshire.

Department for Education and Skills (2000*) Establishing the Connexions Service in Schools (Circular 0302/2000).* London: Department for Education and Skills.

Department for Education and Skills (2001a) *Excellence in Cities: Good practice guidelines for learning mentors.* London: Department for Education and Skills.

Department for Education and Skills (2001b) *Implementing Connexions in Schools (Circular 033/2001)*. London: Department for Education and Skills.

Department for Education and Skills (2002) *Working with Connexions (Circular 0019/2002)*. London: Department for Education and Skills.

Department for Education and Skills (2003a) *Every Child Matters*. London: HM Treasury.

Department for Education and Skills (2003b) *Careers Education and Guidance in England: A national framework 11–19 (Circular 0163/2003)*. London: Department for Education and Skills.

Department for Education and Skills (2004a) *National Occupational Standards for Learning, Development and Support Services*. London: Department for Education and Skills.

Department for Education and Skills (2004b) *Working Together*. London: Department for Education and Skills.

Department for Education and Skills (2005) *Primary National Strategy. Developing Children's Social, Emotional and Behavioural Skills: A whole curriculum approach*. London: Department for Education and Skills

Goleman, D (1995) *Emotional Intelligence*. London: Bloomsbury.

National Children's Bureau (2003) *Developing A Whole School Approach to PSHE and Citizenship*. London: National Children's Bureau.

National Foundation for Educational Research (2003) *Interim Evaluation Reports on Excellence in Cities*. Slough: National Foundation for Educational Research.

National Healthy School Standard (2004a) *Promoting Children and Young People's Participation through the National Healthy School Standard*. London: Health Development Agency.

National Healthy School Standard (2004b) *Promoting Emotional Health and Well-being through the National Healthy School Standard.* London: Health Development Agency.

Office for Standards in Education (2003a) *Excellence in Cities and Education Action Zones: Management and impact.* London: Ofsted.

Office for Standards in Education (2003b) *Standards and Quality 2002/03: Annual Report of Her Majesty's Chief Inspector of Schools.* London: Ofsted.

Office for Standards in Education (2004) *Annual Report of Her Majesty's Chief Inspector of Schools 2003/04.* London: Office for Standards in Education.

Spalding, B and Neilly, J (2004) *Actively Making Connexions Work.* Liverpool: Liverpool City of Learning Mentors.

Young Adult Learners Partnership on behalf of the Connexions Service National Unit (2003) *Explaining Personal and Social Development, DfES Research Report RR480.* London: Department of Education and Skills.

Index